W9-CAL-566

# Ocean
## HABITATS

BY MIRELLA S. MILLER

Published by The Child's World®
1980 Lookout Drive • Mankato, MN 56003-1705
800-599-READ • www.childsworld.com

Acknowledgments
The Child's World®: Mary Berendes, Publishing Director
Red Line Editorial: Editorial direction
The Design Lab: Design
Amnet: Production

Photographs ©: Rich Carey/Shutterstock Images, cover,
1, 18; Eric Isselee/Shutterstock Images, back cover;
Shutterstock Images, back cover, 6–7; Digital Vision, 5,
20–21; Incredible Arctic/Shutterstock Images, 8; Zacarias
Pereira da Mata/Shutterstock Images, 10–11; Richard
Whitcombe/Shutterstock Images, 13; Mike Bauer/
Shutterstock Images, 14; Mogens Trolle/Shutterstock
Images, 16–17; Four Oaks/Shutterstock Images, 22

ISBN 9781623239879
LCCN 2013947273

Printed in the United States of America
Mankato, MN
December, 2013
PA02192

# Table of Contents

# Welcome to the Ocean!

Oceans make up most of Earth's surface. They are big bodies of salt water. An ocean circles each continent. Oceans are full of life. Many plants grow on the ocean floor. There are also special animals that call the ocean home.

Plants and animals work together to live. Animals use plants as food and as homes. Smaller animals use plants to hide from larger animals. **Predators** eat other animals.

The world's oceans are in danger. Changes in the weather are making oceans warmer. It is also causing the water to rise. Human activities also affect oceans. People throw trash and other waste in the water. These activities put plants and animals in danger.

*The ocean floor is filled with plant and animal life.*

# Where Are the World's Oceans?

All of Earth's oceans are connected. This means there is one global ocean. Scientists sort the ocean into five areas. The Pacific Ocean is the largest ocean. It makes up nearly half of Earth's water. The Pacific Ocean is around 17 countries. This includes Australia.

The second largest ocean is the Atlantic Ocean. It is half the size of the Pacific Ocean. The Atlantic Ocean borders North and South America. It also borders Europe and Africa. The Atlantic Ocean connects to the Arctic Ocean in the north. The Arctic Ocean is the smallest ocean.

*Oceans make up much of Earth's surface.*

**North America**

**Pacific Ocean**

The Southern Ocean also connects to the Atlantic Ocean. The Southern Ocean flows around Antarctica.

The Indian Ocean is between Africa, Asia, and Australia. It is the third largest ocean in the world.

The Atlantic Ocean covers 20 percent of Earth's surface.

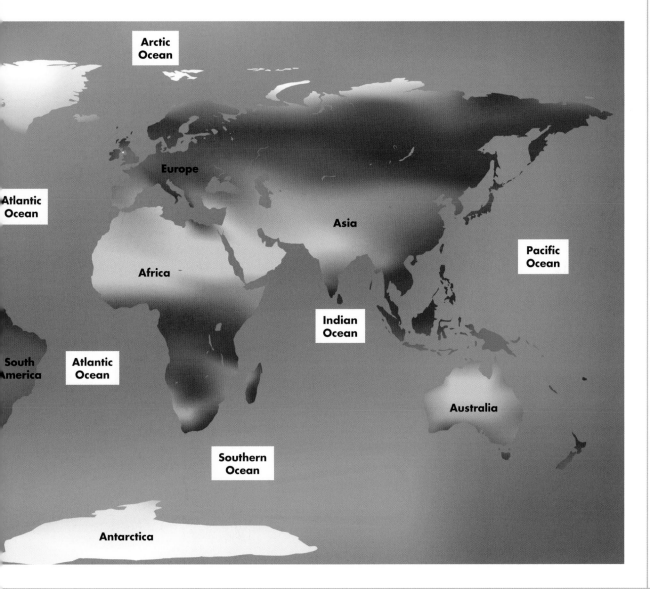

# What Do Oceans Look Like?

The ocean floor has different kinds of **terrain**. It can be rocky or sandy. It can also rise into a volcano or turn into a deep, dark **trench**. The Arctic Ocean and the Southern Ocean both have ice, too.

Sunlight cannot reach the deepest parts of the ocean floor. The water looks black at this level. Animals that live here are used to no sunlight. No plants live here. The middle area of the ocean receives very little sunlight. The water here looks dark blue or black. Plants do not grow here either. Animals such as crabs and eels live in this area of the ocean.

The top level of the ocean receives most of the sunlight. The water can be clear or cloudy. This area of the ocean is full of plant and animal life. Seaweed and kelp are two plants that grow here. **Mammals**, fish, and sea turtles are seen swimming on the top level.

*The Arctic Ocean is covered in ice.*

# Ocean Weather

Not all oceans have warm, sunny weather. Some oceans are cold and dark. The Arctic Ocean has cold weather all year. It rains and snows during the summer months. The Southern Ocean's water is very cold. The Southern Ocean also has the strongest winds ever recorded on Earth.

Other oceans are warm. The Indian, Atlantic, and Pacific Oceans all have storm seasons. Big waves can cause damage to the land closest to these oceans.

*Cities that are near oceans can be damaged during bad storm seasons.*

Since the early 1950s, tropical storms have been given names. Both male and female names are used.

# The Plants of the Ocean

Most ocean plants are a form of **algae**. Algae float and stick to rocks and reefs. Some animals eat algae to survive. Plankton plants are the smallest form of algae. They are food for many animals, including whales.

> Worms, snails, crabs, jellyfish, and fish live in kelp forests. They eat the kelp and use it to hide.

Kelp is another plant that grows in colder waters. Some kelp plants grow to be very big. They grow upward looking for sunlight. Many animals do not eat kelp. They use the kelp forests as homes.

Sea grass also grows on the ocean floor. It grows very thick. It is used as a home by many animals. Sea grass normally grows in warmer ocean water. It also grows in shallower water. Sea grass needs sunlight to survive.

*Sea grass can reach the sunlight easier in shallow ocean water.*

# Deep Ocean Animals

Most ocean animals do not live in the deep, dark parts. This can be a hard place to live, with no sunlight. However, animals have learned how to survive here.

The Japanese spider crab has been found as deep as 2,000 feet (600 m) below the ocean's surface. These giant crabs live in holes on the ocean floor. Spider crabs mostly eat algae.

The tube worm is another animal that lives on the ocean floor. These worms live on the edges of ocean **vents**. The vents throw very hot, **toxic** water into the ocean.

Not all deep ocean animals live on the ocean floor. The Pacific viperfish swims the deepest parts of the ocean at 13,000 feet (4,400 m). The stomach of a Pacific viperfish glows. This draws in food. It then uses its sharp teeth to catch the food.

*Tube worms live on the dark ocean floor near vents.*

# Ocean Mammals

Some mammals are warm-blooded. Many mammals live in cold ocean waters. Others live in warm ocean waters.

Leopard seals live in the cold waters of the Southern Ocean. They have a thick layer of fat to keep them warm. Most of their meals come from penguins and shellfish. The seals have powerful jaws and teeth to catch their food.

Humpback whales travel the ocean waters all year. These giant whales have a strong tail fin to help them move through the water. Even though humpback whales are big, they eat small animals. Plankton and small fish are two foods humpback whales eat.

Bottlenose dolphins are some of the smartest animals to swim in the ocean.

*Leopard seals have special bodies to keep them warm in the cold ocean waters.*

They travel in groups through the warm ocean waters. Bottlenose dolphins must go to the ocean surface to breathe. They eat fish, shrimp, and squid.

# The Amazing Octopus

The common octopus lives in warm ocean waters, usually close to land. Octopuses have big heads and eyes. They also have eight arms. If an octopus loses an arm, it will grow back. Octopuses also have powerful jaws that look like beaks. The beak lets go of venom that can hurt the octopuses' **prey**.

Not only are octopuses unusual looking, they are also smart. If octopuses see a predator, they can change their body color. This helps the octopuses match the plants and rocks around them. Sharks, eels, and dolphins will not be able to see an octopus. Octopuses can also shoot out a cloud of black ink. Then they can quickly swim away from their predators.

Octopuses also use this black ink to stop their prey from getting away. Octopuses feed on crabs, crayfish, and mollusks. The black ink keeps them from seeing or running away.

*Octopuses are among the smartest animals swimming in the ocean.*

# Threats to the Ocean

Ocean plants and animals have learned to survive in both cold and warm ocean waters. But changes in the weather and human activities are harming ocean habitats.

One big problem is changes in the weather. This causes the water to become warmer. Warmer water can harm some plants and animals, such as krill. Krill is an important food source for many other animals in the ocean. Warmer temperatures cause ice to melt. This makes ocean water levels rise. Warmer water and higher water levels also lead to stronger storms. Storms can damage ocean life. They can also damage the land closest to the ocean.

Another problem is pollution in oceans. Humans throw garbage and other harmful things in the ocean.

*Fishers must be careful not to take too many fish from the ocean.*

This pollution damages plants and animals. Plants and animals need a clean habitat to survive.

Overfishing in oceans is also a problem. Fishers are taking too many fish out of the ocean too fast. New fish cannot grow as fast as they are being caught. When this happens there is not enough food for other animals. Humans must take care of the ocean so it will always be a safe habitat for the plants and animals who live there.

# GLOSSARY

**algae (AL-jee)** Algae are a plant found in the ocean. Most ocean plants are a form of algae.

**mammals (MAM-uhls)** Mammals are warm-blooded animals. Many ocean mammals live in cold water.

**predators (PRED-uh-turs)** Predators are animals that prey or destroy. Octopuses quickly swim away from predators.

**prey (PRAY)** An animal taken by a predator as food is prey. Octopuses use black ink to stop their prey.

**terrain (tuh-RAYN)** The physical features of land are known as terrain. The ocean floor has different terrain.

**toxic (TOK-sik)** If something is toxic, it is poisonous. Ocean vents let toxic water into the ocean.

**trench (TRENCH)** A trench is a long, narrow, steep-sided ditch in the ocean floor. There are parts of the ocean floor that turn into a trench.

**vents (VENTS)** A vent is an opening for gas or liquid to escape. Tubeworms live near ocean vents.

# TO LEARN MORE

## BOOKS

Benoit, Peter. *Oceans*. New York: Scholastic, 2011.

Owen, Ruth. *Octopuses*. New York: Rosen Publishing, 2012.

Sill, Cathryn P. *About Habitats*: *Oceans*. Atlanta: Peachtree Publishing, 2012.

## WEB SITES

Visit our Web site for links about ocean habitats:
**childsworld.com/links**

*Note to Parents, Teachers, and Librarians: We routinely verify our Web links to make sure they are safe and active sites. So encourage your readers to check them out!*

# INDEX

## ABOUT THE AUTHOR

Mirella S. Miller lives in Minnesota. She does not live near the ocean, but it is one of her favorite places to visit.